To Jea

FROM VISIONS OF GRANDEUR - TO DEPTHS OF DESPAIR

Help! Is Anyone Out There?

By

Norma Lou Johnson

Lou Johnson

1 – 2 7 10

Copyright © 2009 by Norma Lou Johnson

From Visions of Grandeur - To Depths of Despair
Help! Is Anyone Out There?
by Norma Lou Johnson

Printed in the United States of America

ISBN 9781615793006

Unless otherwise indicated, Bible quotations are taken from
The King James Version of the Bible.

www.xulonpress.com

God bless you, Jean –

DEDICATION

To my beautiful Daughter, for whom I would erase
all of the pain if only it were humanly possible.
What a brave survivor you are as you have
struggled, even to this present day, to make sense of
it all.
To the memory of my late Husband and our two
Sons, each of whom left this life far too early. While
their lives were not long, each was fully lived.

TABLE OF CONTENTS

Introduction

There she was, looking directly into the camera,
"We're not buying it! The bi-polar explanation is
just a cop-out excuse!!"
The nation's most popular female
talk show host had listened
incredulously to her guest share from
first-hand knowledge
how a here-to-fore respectable loved one behaved in
a deranged manner
due to a chemical imbalance.
My heart sank as this acclaimed and influential host
then declared, "There is
no such thing as bi-polar chemical disorder."
Why should this bother me so?

Chapter 1

The Phone Call
That Changed Everything

"What?" "What?," I screamed into the telephone each time Rafael said it: "Leon died this morning." The 6:30 a.m. phone call jarred me out of a sound, peaceful sleep.

The day before I had managed to get my husband, Leon, admitted into a mental hospital in Zacatecas, Mexico. When I saw that the strong medication had calmed him down, and that his body was relaxing on the hospital bed, I returned to our house in Calera. Emotionally and physically weary, I welcomed a blissful sleep - free from frightening encounters with a wild-eyed, mentally disturbed husband.

Just twelve hours later the hospital staff, knowing I had a neighbor who spoke good English, called Rafael to convey the news that Leon was found dead on his bed when they made their early morning rounds. I simply could not believe I would be hearing such devastating words as I sat on the edge of my bed, alone in a strange country we had only recently moved to.

I finally got up, opened my front door and screamed out: "Why aren't you here with me? Why am I all alone?" It seemed to take a long time before their front door opened and Rafael and his mother walked across the street to try to comfort me. "You must call your children," they kept telling me. "No, I can't tell my children. I can't call them." They finally got through to me that this was exactly what I must do, and they stood by until I had contacted my two sons in Oregon and my daughter in Arizona.

"I'll go get a shower, Norma, and will be back to take you to the hospital," said Rafael. Somehow I managed to get myself ready, and soon we were making the thirty-minute drive to Zacatecas.

This time I did not have to walk down the long corridors, pass through one locked area and into another. No, Leon's body lay in a small, candlelight filled room near the hospital entrance. Crucifixes, Madonnas, artificial flowers, green lighting and many candles made for a somewhat garish atmosphere.

A nurse waiting for me to identify the body stood quietly by until I began to touch my beloved, sobbing, "Leon, oh my precious Leon." The staff left me to grieve privately.

An autopsy reported that he died of a brain hemorrhage. My thinking is that in the hours preceding hospitalization, hyper mania caused his blood pressure to sky-rocket. Indeed, he had been babbling incoherently. His head seemed to be on fire and he had been constantly searching for cold water to pour over himself.

Rafael, as well as the dear people from his church, rallied around to assist me in the many details of preparing to return to America. I simply could not conceive of adjusting to life in an unfamiliar country, struggling with a new language, and facing the loss of my Leon.

The Lord saw to it that I was never alone. Rafael stayed by my side throughout the entire ordeal of identifying the body, waiting for the autopsy, receiving the medical reports, arranging for cremation, and helping me choose a wooden container to carry the ashes.

With a heavy heart I piled almost everything we had brought to Mexico back into our '93 Hyundai, and dear Rafael drove me to El Paso where my sister had flown to meet me. Rafael then took the seventeen hour bus ride back to his home, and Lora Mae and I drove on to her home in Los Angeles. Soon my children arrived, entering the bedroom where I sat clutching in a box all that remained of their departed father.

Chapter 2

A Godly Heritage

I grew up in a God-honoring home, learning - along with my elder sister, elder brother and younger brother - the Bible and the Christian way to live. Family fun times hold dear memories: breathlessly watching Oakland's Lake Merritt fireworks every July 4; anticipating the annual Shriner's Circus; bragging to everyone about Mom's theme and fun-filled birthday parties; hosting dinners and housing traveling quartets and missionaries; loading up Daddy's car to take us and our friends to Saturday night Youth for Christ; traveling in the old family car together, (with Mother supplying wonderful car game activities); and the highlight of every summer - spending one week at Family Bible Camp in the Santa Cruz mountains.

At the tender age of three and a half I asked Jesus to come live in my heart. I can recall it clearly today – three quarters of a century later! Most of my growing up years were in the Evangelical Free Church of America, yet it is my parents whom I credit for taking seriously their respon- sibility to teach me in the ways of the Lord. They were also very strict in those days. No "worldly" influences. No attending movies, no television, and use of radio was very limited so as not to listen to "worldly" music. I did enjoy hearing the "Henry Aldrich" show while doing my after-school ironing chore. No lipstick, no open toe shoes, no earrings, no pedal pushers (windy day picnic? – apparently a windblown skirt was more holy than wearing the forbidden "pants").

Lastly, but most certainly, NO dating of unsaved boys and/or Pentecostal boys. Funny, but Daddy grouped these two together back then. That rule was difficult, because it seeemd that the local Assembly of God guys I saw at Youth for Christ were definitely the cutest ones around.

After graduating from high school, I followed my brother Robert to Prairie Bible Institute in Three Hills, Alberta Canada. A year later my parents sold the family home in Richmond, California and joined the staff of "PBI," enrolling my "little brother" David in the corresponding high school. All of the Bible teaching I had learned from my parents was now being reinforced even more thoroughly at this fine school.

During missions conference in my senior year, I responded to a Regions Beyond Missionary Union representative, Ebenezer Vine, when he made a plea for helpers. However, during our interview he pointed out that I would first need to pursue either teaching or nursing as at that time countries were accepting only people with a professional degree.

So upon graduation from Bible School, I enrolled at Trinity Seminary and Bible College in Chicago (now in Deerfield, IL) and pursued a degree in Elementary Education. I then applied to the denomination's missions department to teach missionarys' children in Caracas, Venezuela. But now the respresentative, H. G. Rhodine, said I would need to first get some stateside teaching experience before coming to the field. With that, I returned to my home, the San Francisco Bay Area, and completed five years of elementary teaching.

All this while, a great longing began to grow in my heart to be married to a fine Christian man who would love Jesus even more than he loved me. Marriage to a non-believer was totally out of the question. But after graduation from Prairie Bible Institute, followed 3 years later by graduation from Chicago's Trinity Seminar and Bible College, "Mr. Right" had not come along.

"Come on, Norma, go with me to Mt. Hermon for the Navigator's Conference. I don't want to drive alone," said my childhood friend Shirley. I was not interested in such a trip. As 4th grade school teacher in Alameda, I wanted to spend that weekend preparing bulletin boards for my class-room. However, Shirley was convincing, and we arrived in time for the morning session in the large tabernacle.

Entering the dining room for lunch, I observed a roomful of good looking young men. Testing my recent commitment to do nothing to help God find me a husband, I let Shirley lead us to a table, and we began a conversation with an older couple. My curiosity was suddenly piqued as I heard a clear, resonant male voice nearby mention a Christian Servicemen's Center that was of interest to me. As I turned to match the voice with the person, I saw a handsome sailor who was sharing how he had met the Lord Jesus at Oakland's "Port 'O Call."

"Uh, excuse me," but how long have you been a Christian?," I asked. I had the idea that sailors went to that center, met some pretty girls, said a few "words," but never got serious about salvation. As Leon J. Rendell turned to me, face aglow, I looked into the most beautiful pair of blue eyes I had ever seen. He replied, "That was four years ago." "Oh," was about all I could manage, turning back to my girlfriend and our lunch. Our little encounter left a deep impression on me since he was so very full of joy about his conversion – yes, so excited – and he had a genuine sparkle about him. That it had taken place as long as four years ago intrigued me.

I left the dining room to browse in the bookstore and check out the newest music. Suddenly I was startled to hear a pleasant "Hi!" Looking up into his kind, blue eyes, I sensed a surge of warmth and joy. Within moments we realized we had an instant connection in music. I learned that he sang, and he learned that I played the piano.

Soon it was time for the afternoon session to begin, but Shirley decided we needed to head on back home at that point. Unbeknownst to me, Leon, who had been assigned to usher in that service, had gone up and down the aisles looking for me.

Three weeks later, another friend asked me to attend a Friday night Easter presentation at Neighborhood Church in Oakland. This was a very large building built on the round with the balcony having many different exits to the main floor. With hundreds of people attending, somehow Leon and I spotted each other from a great distance in the balcony. He told me later that his buddy kept nudging him saying, "She's looking at you again," and of course I would then quickly turn away.

The service concluded and each of us exited down a different stairwell but somehow found ourselves on the ground level eyeball to eyeball. We were both beaming, and I asked if he would like to bring some of the sailors off his ship (USS Midway) to my apartment. I told him that my roommate Janie and I would invite some girlfriends over for an evening of singing and fellowship. The date was set for the following Monday. The evening came and went – no sailors!

The next day I posed a question to Jimmy, one of my students, whose Daddy was stationed aboard the USS Midway. He replied that the ship went out to sea for a week. The following Friday night a very embarrassed Leon called to apologize. Now when I am real happy I often fall into rather spirited laughter. Leon interpreted my laughing as being silly and was afraid to come over. He did not want to waste an evening on a giggling airhead! So he tested me by asking me to give him my spiritual testimony. That's Leon! He just wanted to be sure I really knew the Lord before making the date.

Apparently whatever I said was the right thing, because we both believe it was that very night while spending hour after hour at my piano bench singing favorite gospel songs, getting acquainted, that we fell in love. It seems that he and I fell in love around JESUS. From our first meeting on April 6 to our engagement on May 30, we "waited" until August 17 to get married – all in the year 1963.

Leon's love for his precious Lord Jesus initially caught my attention, but I later observed that this also remained his most outstanding quality throughout our marriage. Our beautiful wedding took place four months later. Taking my hands and gazing lovingly into my eyes, he sang:

Together, with Jesus, life's pathway we tread,
As one heart united by His hand are lead;
His love e'er surrounds us, His comfort and cheer
Will ever sustain us, tho days may be drear.

Together, with Jesus, we live for His praise,
And pray that His sunshine may gladden our ways,
What God joins together, none other can break,
Yea, blessed the union that Jesus doth make.

Together, with Jesus, constrained by His love,
We seek for the lost ones, and point them above,
From valleys of service to mountains of rest,
He guides us and keeps us, in Him we are blest.

Together with Him, oh love so divine.
Together with Him, oh rapture sublime.
Together with Him, life's pathway we tread.

That was the happiest day of my life. If anybody had tried to tell me that I would be living a hell on earth two decades later, I would not have believed it. The first verse of our wedding song alludes to the possibility of "dreary days," but I could not possibly conceive of the horrors yet to come. In my wildest dreams I could never imagine that it would end so tragically!

Chapter 3

Triangle:
Secret to a Great Marriage

Leon's yearning to explore the Bible and search out every possible hidden truth was evidenced in the hours he spent reading and studying. I was often reminded of the triangle he drew during our engagement period. "Jesus" at top, "Leon" at left, and "Norma" at right. "You see, Honey, as you and I move closer to Jesus, you and I will become closer to each other." With both of us having a keen desire to please our Lord, it is not surprising that Leon and I really did enjoy a loving oneness.

After only three months of marriage, Leon's ship went on a Westpac cruise. Since I chose to withdraw my money from California State Teacher's Retirement, I was able to meet his ship at every overseas port. While thousands of wives and girlfriends stood at the pier in Oakland waving goodbye to their sailor men, I was happily shouting, "See you in Subic Bay!" Indeed, the ship no sooner sailed off than my parents drove me to the airport where I flew into Honolulu for a little visit and then on to the Philippines. As a "seagull" (term for wives who follow the ships) I was able to spend time with missionary friends I had gone to Bible school with as well as meet some new friends. I worked with Wycliffe in Manilla, an orphange in Sasebo Japan, helped Evangelical Free Church missionries in Hong Kong, and did secretarial work at the Overseas Christian Servicemen's Center in Olongapo (Subic Bay) Philippines.

One day in November of 1963 I was visiting dear PBI Wycliffe missionary friends who lived in a nipa hut and who, along with the natives, used the dirty nearby river to bathe and to do laundry. I had just completed my own bath right alongside carabaos (water buffalo) and women washing laundry and was climbing the steps to the hut when my friend met me with ashen face. She said, "Norma, it is terrible. Les just heard over the short wave that President Kennedy was assasinated". Very strange being off in that far land when such a dramatic incident was taking place in my homeland.

A few weeks later, Leon's orders sent him back to America. The timing was perfect, in that I had by now used up almost all of my travel funds. It was good to be together and back in California.

The United States Navy took good care of us those first four years together. Our three children were born and received their "first year checkups," all courtesy of the USN. Leon had served four years with the Navy before meeting me, and then another four as a married man. It appeared to make good sense for him to carry on for twelve more years so as to enjoy the military's excellent twenty year retirement program.

But it was not to be. In July of 1967, Leon became a civilian. To give up this plumb of early retirement in order to prepare for Christian ministry did not seem odd to us. I was so proud of my dedicated, godly husband, and when he expressed such a desire I heartily agreed. My parents voiced their concerns for our future welfare, but we could only think of this decision as living out the Psalms 34:3

verse written on the little white Bible that topped our wedding cake:

"LET US EXALT HIS NAME TOGETHER."

But perhaps this decision should have been our first signal of a problem called "Bi-polar Chemical Disorder." We had not yet heard this term, nor had we heard the term, "visions of grandeur."

With the encouragement of Jessie Miller, founding Director of Overseas Christian Servicemen's Center, we moved to Colorado and Leon enrolled at Western Bible Institute (later known as Colorado Christian University). Our sites were now set on preparing to some day operate a home away from home for overseas military personnel.

I recall those years with great joy, thinking myself to be the happiest, proudest wife and mother alive! But I did not understand why I would sometimes find my husband in the depths of despondency. He would be ready to drop out of school, but would eventually start to come out of the depression. Later, Leon would brag on me to others, saying how I helped him get over these periods.

Had we heard the term "Manic-Depression?" No.

Do I wonder now if "Manic Depression" is what Leon was experiencing? Yes.

Leon attended college while holding down some part time jobs, the first one serving as a Youth Pastor. He seemed to function very well as Bible teacher to the teens, as well as in structuring their church related social and recreational activities. Leon then went on to serve as Associate Pastor of a large church in Colorado. He wore two "hats": Director of the single adult department and Director of Evangelism.

There were never any incidents, other than the depression episodes, that made one suspect he might be operating in an unbalanced mode during these years of special ministry. He graduated with honors from Bible school and received a Bachelor of Biblical Education degree, after which he became ordained to the gospel ministry.

So far, we seemed to function in a beautifully balanced "normal" mode. Certainly Leon was highly respected and valued for his excellence in Christian ministries. "He lives in our home what you hear him preach from the pulpit." was my consistent response to those who expressed their admiration and appreciation for my husband.

By this time, we were no longer anticipating following through with the overseas servicemen's center "call." Rather, we purchased our first home and began remodeling the basement for extra bedrooms. We were truly happy, fulfilled, and appeared to be a "normal" Christian couple anticipating the future together.

Chapter 4

Some Called It The Gypsy Life

So what would prompt Leon, in 1973, to sell our furnishings and home we had lived in for only one year, take our seven, eight and nine year old children, move into a borrowed camper with what was now left of our entire earthly belongings, travel across the United States with "the Jesus people," and eventually move to Sweden to serve as Team Leader for a European traveling tent caravan? When the opportunity came to sell our home, uproot the family and begin traveling throughout several eastern states with a mobile group called Christ is the Answer, teaching the Bible to ex-hippies, preaching under the big tent, and being a liaison between this mobile group and local pastors, Leon was willing and ready. I, too, found this very exciting as I had wanted to be a missionary from early childhood.

Our three young children continued their schooling, being taught by certified former public school teachers who now traveled with the group. Campers had been made into traveling classrooms, and the children had a marvelous time together.

When our caravan had reached the East Coast, it had grown so large in numbers that the leader wanted Leon to move to Goteborg, Sweden and establish a home base for a new, European travel team. So Leon went on ahead, found housing for all of us, and soon sent for our family as well as a mini-team who would stay with us at home base.

What fun it was for our little family to set up house-keeping in our new flat in Sweden. The children got enrolled in an international school within walking distance where children came from many countries and learned to speak only Swedish. They picked up the language very quickly.

While in Sweden our family had the privilege of spending a few weeks in Rome with the travel team. We found this time most refreshing since we had been exposed to unbelievably graphic street pornography as well as the constant presence of drunken men in the Goteborg streets. Leon loved preaching in the nightly tent rallies as well as in some of the churches of Rome. He even got to board the USS Guam and some other ships stationed in Naples and made arrangements for the team band to go aboard to preach and to sing.

One great joy was when Leon met Joe, a former pimp, in Amsterdam's notorious red-light district. Joe had become a Christian and was now out on the streets witnessing for Jesus. He happily announced, "I need no longer go around with a gun."

He also had the very unique experience of receiving a personal audience with King Carl Gustav on the King's 29th birthday. When the interview was completed, Leon was led to a special balcony to observe as King Carl was led out to another balcony where thousands of his subjects greeted him, along with an impressive display of horses.

Another heady experience was when Leon and some team members came aboard a Russian ship docked in

Goteborg and had the joy of singing songs about Jesus to some shocked Russian Naval officers.

Leon's life was profoundly changed while living in Sweden when he was invited to take a brief trip to Israel. He returned from his days in the Holy Land with a keen desire to go back with a ministry team. It seemed that the main focus of his prayers, sermons, Bible teachings, efforts, time and energies from then on was to bless Israel. A favorite quote was from Genesis 12:3. The Lord told Abram: "I will bless those who bless you.' This was God's word, and such truth was not to be denied.

Restlessness? Flight of ideas? Or were we hearing and obeying the will of God?

After only two years with this mobile ministry team, we felt it important to leave and return to life in America. To many folk, our decision may have appeared as either of the first two options. However, the fact is that Leon and I were growing increasingly uncomfortable with signs we observed that indicated the CITA movement was heading scripturally and morally off base. Leon discreetly went to the team's founder/leader to discuss these issues, but his concerns were not received as valid.

Quietly, then, our little family of five packed a few belongings (two suitcases each) and boarded a plane to Boulder, Colorado where we had been invited to live temporarily in the home of a family friend. Before long we were able to move into a rental, and we rejoiced once again as God provided all of the furniture, kitchen needs, bedding, etc., that we needed.

Chapter 5

The Vision Intensified

L eon's energy and grandiose vision seemed to have no boundaries. While working various part-time jobs, he found ways to do what he loved best. He coordinated the "Here's Life" evangelistic program for our area, opened up three Christian Coffee House ministries, wrote and produced some prophetic type tracts, served as an associate in a neighborhood church, founded Bless Israel Now, International (a ministry majoring in teaching believers how to bless the Jewish people) and began training teams to go to Israel to walk not just <u>where </u>Jesus walked, but AS Jesus walked.

Dividing into pairs, the trained teams saw not only the special sights of Israel, but they also found ways to speak with Israelis, telling them, "We are Christians who love you and pray for your peace." This approach usually prompted an amazed response from not only the "sabras" (Israeli-born Jews) but also the Jewish tourists. They seemed to expect disdain from us, believing that Christians considered Jews to be Christ-Killers. The trained team members had the joy of pointing out that it was their own personal sins that sent Jesus to the cross, not the work of the Jewish people.

Leon's passion for God's chosen people was genuine, and he envisioned beautiful buildings being erected that would result in ways and means to demonstrate to them God's great love.

I was totally convinced during those years that my husband was one of the most dedicated Christians on planet earth. I still believe that! What I did not consider was the possibility of his having a chemical imbalance that manifested itself in grandiose notions, delusions, periods of perceived self-importance and empowerment, impaired judgment, and numerous other disruptive symptoms.

So what do you think, reader? Does all this sound like the work of a mentally disturbed man? I certainly did not think so.

What about Raymond, Eugene and Sharnelle, now ages eleven, twelve and thirteen? What were they thinking? It pained my heart when I later learned that at this point they felt neglected by their father. From their own perspective, Leon was wholly immersed in his ministry visions, to the exclusion of bonding with them - his own children.

And me? I was totally immersed in adoration and admiration of my precious husband, and apparently unable to see how the children were feeling – neglected by a dad who had his parental priorities out of line! Only God can know the agony of my soul today to learn what those dear young ones were beginning to feel – and would continue to feel for the rest of their lives!!

Chapter 6

Are We Having Fun Yet?

Leon strongly urged me to consider going to Israel with him on his 3rd tour, and I finally consented after the money for my trip was unexpectedly provided. As a result of my spending time in the land, getting caught up (in a lesser measure) with Leon's excitement and love for Israel, we decided in 1978 to move to Jerusalem. Our goal was to better understand and relate to the Jewish people.

Thus it was that on September 18, 1978, after once again selling everything we owned and carrying only two suitcases apiece, we five Rendell's flew first to Sweden where Christian friends had arranged housing and speaking engagements in several churches. There we met many Swedish believers who also had a love for Israel and offered much support and encouragement. Indeed, a Christian car dealer gave us a beautiful 1971 Volvo station wagon!

A chaplain friend stationed at Baumholder, Germany contacted us while we were in Sweden to see if Leon would come be the speaker for their Thanksgiving Servicemen's Conference. What a glorious two weeks we had at that base and also touring the area.

From there we drove down into Italy at the invitation of some believers we had met while ministering with the Christ is the Answer travel team. Leon was thrilled to preach through interpreters, and the loving Christians of Rome provided gracious hospitality for our family. How amazed we were as Sister Gaetano sat us down to what we thought was a pasta dinner, only to discover that this was simply the first of several courses. Our eyes and our tummies seemed to get bigger and bigger as she kept appearing from the kitchen bearing more platters of delicious foods.

In the home of our hosts, we had to rely on sign language as they spoke no English and we spoke no Italian. It got to be a lot of fun when we discovered that we could carry on a "conversation" by finding scriptures in each other's Bibles. For instance, I found Philippians 4:19 to convey that GOD would be supplying all of our needs as we continued our journey into Israel. Sister Gaetano read it from her Bible, threw up her hands and shouted "Hallelujah!" while we laughed and hugged.

This form of communication reminds me of the young minister who wanted to meet an attractive young girl. Being bashful, he did not know how to approach her. So he opened the hymnal to page 179, "I Need Thee Every Hour," and handed it to her. But she found page 277 and showed him, "God Will Take Care of You."

Continuing on our journey, we came to Pireaus, Greece where we drove our Volvo on to a ferry and enjoyed sailing over to beautiful Haifa, finally arriving in the land of Israel on December 8. The first few days in the land we stayed in Bethlehem at the home of an elderly lady who had been ministering there for many years. She was loving, helpful and encouraging. How faithfully the Lord led us as we were soon able to rent a most adequate apartment in Jerusalem located quite close to the Jerusalem Theater.

The children began attending "ulpan," a language school. While the two youngest caught on to the Hebrew language very quickly, it was extremely difficult for our eldest. We were all happy when there was an opening at the Anglican School in Jerusalem for them to continue their studies with English speaking teachers and friends.

I went happily about my housekeeping duties. However, I discovered this task was far more difficult in Jerusalem than in the USA! Housecleaning was a challenge, as we lived on a hill surrounded by a lot of dust. Grocery shopping was a daily event. A brightly colored woven basket in each hand, I would walk along the dusty hillside to find the nearest market. Choosing fresh vegetables, fruit, milk and meat I would then return home to prepare the evening's meat.

Leon began writing a saga of our family's involvement with Israel. It became published and served to motivate Gentile believers to support Israel. This book was also an effective tool to assure our Jewish friends of our concern for their well being. It was a great joy to explain that the One we follow, Jesus of Nazareth, was also a Jew and that scriptures reveal He is indeed their Messiah.

I will never forget the middle age clerk at the Jerusalem market where I shopped. I always tried to avoid her line, for she seemed so angry and impatient when I would get confused with the currency. But tears come to my eyes even now as I recall Israel's Day of Remembrance, when sirens are heard all over the city, every motion comes to a halt, and for sixty seconds Israelis remember their war dead. That day I found myself, uncomfortably, in her line. But when that siren went off and the market became suddenly still and quiet, I noticed that she began to sob, left her station and hurried to the back room. Never again did I try to avoid her line. I went home that day and told my family, "Give her an extra loving smile. She is deeply wounded by all she has lost because of the wars. She sees us, Christians, as Jew haters. We must show her much love."

Meanwhile, Leon's smiles turned to tears of despair. What could have happened? The man who was on such a "high" with choosing to live in Israel, wanting to write a book, enjoying such visions of ministry with God's chosen people, was now spending entire days literally sobbing and wanting to return to America. I could not believe it! I thought we would be living in that land for the rest of our earthly days.

Still: No clue whatsoever about "chemical imbalance." The only framework from which I seemed to be able to process things was "spiritual." Surely the Lord had all the answers for these "downers," didn't He? Then why did my beloved husband continue to cry every day? I felt helpless and began to agree with him that we needed to leave Israel. I had concluded that he was not adjusting to the language barrier and the cultural changes.

Sharnelle took the announcement of our moving back to America the hardest. She is our "linguist." Three years earlier, while living in Sweden, she had attended a school for foreigners who came from many other countries. The only language spoken by the teacher was Swedish. Little Sharnelle picked up not only perfect Swedish, but also the exact dialog of Goteborg, the city we lived in. This was evidenced one day while she played at a nearby park. Running over to where I sat observing on a bench, she exclaimed rather indignantly, "Mamma, see that old lady sitting over there? She will not believe that I am from America. She says I speak perfect Swedish. Now you have to go over there and convince her I am from America!" I had to speak less than one sentence in my broken Swedish before the woman believed my daughter was an American. But until then, with Sharnelle's blonde pigtails, blue eyes, little black clogs and perfect command of the language, the woman had remained skeptical.

And now, this same little linguist had mastered the Hebrew language, and by her twelfth birthday in the land she was not only speaking it fluently, but actually thinking in Hebrew. Sharnelle had literally fallen in love with Israel.

But back to America we moved in 1979 (a mere seven months later) to the sorrow of at least one child, but to the great joy of our eldest. Through an amazing set of circumstances, we were able to purchase a lovely home. Our children re-enrolled in the local schools, meeting up once again with the youth they had started grade school with. Leon found employment in the secular field, and I delved happily into "keeping" the home.

Chapter 7

What About The Children?

"He's the best!" "What a great Bible teacher your husband is!" "Leon has such a command of the scriptures." "I love to hear him preach."

These and many other such comments filled my heart with wifely pride. Up to now, all of Leon's enthusiasm, fervor and commitment for things of God were viewed upon by the Christian community as admirable qualities. However, now in hindsight – and to my great sorrow – I have accepted the fact that our children continued to feel neglected by a dad who had his parental priorities out of line.

Leon believed his purpose in returning to America was to encourage believers there to stand by Israel. He was invited into many circles to share his message, including being invited by the Rabbi into a Jewish synagogue! Leon worked very closely with this same Rabbi and the Jewish National Fund to encourage Christians to raise money for planting trees in Israel.

As my husband's passion and love for Israel began to escalate, so did an urgency having to do with "End Times." He turned our basement room into a "bomb shelter" because he believed the end was approaching and we would be enduring the first part of a tribulation period upon this earth. Leon urgently related all of his "revelations" of coming disaster and demanded that we prepare for them. We had to go through practice sessions, all fitting awkwardly under a makeshift "bomb shelter." He spoke with great authority, appearing to be super alert to what was about to happen. The entire family had to help him store great quantities of water, food and other survival materials. It was during this period that I, his adoring wife, finally began to become uneasy with what I was seeing and hearing.

It was also during this time that our precious children were into their teen/high school years. These dear ones were having to deal with all of the changes and pressures of that stage while observing bizarre behavior from their dad. Unwisely, in my longing to see the children accept, love and respect their father, I went into a mode of trying to defend his strangeness. How I wish now that I had understood how devastating this was for the children. Why didn't I, instead, concentrate on getting into their hearts and heads and feeling with them all of their embarrassment, shame and confusion? One reason for writing this book is that should a parent with similar circumstances read this they will not repeat my mistakes.

The national elections were coming up, and Leon went full steam working in our neighborhood caucus. He attended all of the political events, meeting with candidates to ask one specific question: "If it came down to getting oil for America or for standing with Israel, which would you choose?" He made it quite clear they would not get his vote if turning against Israel might be an option. This burning passion motivated him to travel to Washington, D.C. in an attempt to meet with President Carter. He did get to meet with a presidential assistant and gave his message of warning that America needs to stand with Israel.

It is important here to bring up the matter of diet. At the time, I did not view his consumption of a commercial weight loss drink as being related to his increasingly strange behavior. But it is interesting to me now that the very powdered protein drink he used, almost to the exclusion of other foods, was later deemed to be extremely harmful and taken off the market. One can only imagine the effect on a person already predisposed to having a chemical imbalance consuming a drink that was found to be harmful to brain chemicals!

Leon was also obsessed with getting his body "in shape for the coming days." While rapidly dropping pounds, he also maintained a very rigid exercise routine. He was very stressed about the situation in the middle east and USA's possible sell-out to the Arabs.

Probably the clearest sign to me of Leon being mentally disturbed was in the building of "Little Israel." I could not understand why he spent hours upon hours digging up the earth in what had been our beautiful back yard. He said he had to build a replica of Jerusalem and that many people would come to see it. Yes, they would even pay to view this creation. He envisioned almost non-stop paid tours during which he would fervently expound on what the Bible has to say about end times and about Israel. To this end, he enlisted our children in spending endless hours of labor on the project. He was consumed with a burning passion to see this completed.

Photos from my album tell the story. Yes, he did have his infamous "Grand Opening." My personal embarrassment on that night is something I cannot forget, and the pictures do not hide the strained expression on my face as I tried so valiantly to keep on believing in my husband.

It was also during these months that the book he began writing while in Jerusalem was published and delivered to our door. Hundreds of large boxes of books! Not paper backs, but 9 x 11 hard covered – because Leon was convinced he had a best seller and that the money was going to begin pouring in. He was also convinced that hundreds of people would read his book and begin to faithfully support Israel in meaningful ways.

With all the furor going on around a man who appeared by now to be "possessed" with Israel and end times, we had three beautiful children trying to find their way into adulthood. And a mother who wanted with all of her heart to see those children believe in their dad. Unrealistic? Yes, I can see it now. Too late!!

Chapter 8

Damage That
Cannot Be Reversed

Nothing could have prepared the children and me for what we witnessed one horrible and unforgettable Saturday night in 1982. Leon had awakened, slipped quietly out of bed, and followed "the voices" that told him to descend the stairs into our basement. Each step, he was "told," had a special spiritual significance. By the time the frightening noises in the basement "bomb shelter" room had awakened the rest of us, Leon was exhibiting extreme psychotic behavior. He was incoherent, his eyes wild and vacant.

At this point I am unable (unwilling?) to recall many details of that night. There is a terrible darkness that I sense just referring to those hours. And my children were so traumatized by it that I do not wish to ask them for their recollections. Suffice it to say, we felt the presence of evil in that room. He told me later that horrible and lewd scenes appeared before him and that there were things he could never tell me. He said he felt as though he had looked straight into the eyes of Satan.

Once again, the only framework I knew to work from was spiritual. I concluded that an evil spirit had come over my husband and therefore it needed to be rebuked. Whatever the case, we did manage to get Leon to eventually make some sense and then return to his bed. We termed this an "attack" and proceeded to our regular church services in the morning.

After church was over we joined a family who had invited us to their home. When dinner was over, Leon began to relate to the hosts what had happened during the night. Suddenly, that look and feeling of sheer evil came over him again, his body became catatonic, and he began using inappropriate speech. The shocked host quickly showed us to the door, and since Leon was obviously unable to drive, I took the wheel.

We never made it home. I felt I had to quickly pull over and stop the car because Leon was scaring us. While our son tried to subdue his father on the city sidewalk, I ran across the street to a telephone and dialed 911. An ambulance arrived, put Leon into a straitjacket, and took him to Boulder General Hospital.

It was very apparent to me that my dear husband was not in his right mind. I was desperate to know what to do. Thinking he might calm down and return to sanity if he could see all of his children, I arranged for them to go down the hall where he was sitting, restrained, on the edge of a gurney. But that was the worst thing I could have done! No child should ever have to hear the evil words that came from his mouth while he was in this condition. I had not expected this, but over twenty years later the repercussions continue and the damage appears irreparable.

What salve is available now for my pain in recalling how I tried so hard to explain away all of the insanity, especially the evil words that were spoken? What comfort is available to me now as I realize the added damage I unwittingly caused by such statements as: "Your daddy didn't mean that. He did not realize what he was saying. He is not an evil man." Why, oh why, did I not instead relate only to their pain rather than use such futile methods to cause them to forgive and understand what was going on. But it is all too late!

My original purpose in writing this book was to help the reader to see that

1. Mental illness is no respecter of persons.
2. It is nothing to be ashamed of.
3. There are helpful ways to minister to the mentally ill.
4. Loved ones of the mentally ill may find strength and encouragement.
5. Loved ones will be able to survive the chaotic aftermath of mental illness.
6. It is important to separate the person from the sickness.

How helpful it would have been to me, dear reader, if back in 1982 when Leon's condition first manifested I would have been handed a book about mental illness - or if someone would have come forward to say, "I understand; I know what is happening; there is help available." How I needed someone to walk alongside me. Instead I was met by bewildered, frustrated friends who had never seen such strange behavior. Now, as a mentor ahead on a path, I seek to provide invaluable support to those walking behind.

Interesting, isn't it, how our 20/20 vision is often quite clear in hindsight? Early on, I did not suspect – nor would have understood – such terms as "bi-polar disorder." I had never heard of such a thing as "chemical imbalance" but the following character changes I began to notice were indeed puzzling to me.

1. periods of severe, prolonged depression
2. low self-esteem
3. resistance and unwillingness to share with a counselor
4. restlessness with frequent flight of ideas for life changes
5. violent outbursts
6. anger which sometimes resulted in physical damage of household objects or persons
7. reticence or unwillingness to reveal deep hurts from his childhood
8. frequent inability to sleep due to flight of ideas
9. unteachable attitude and conveying he was final authority on all matters
10. often saying he would commit suicide if not for me, his wife

The first time I saw Leon deeply depressed was in November of 1967. He would sit tearfully for long periods of time looking very sullen. I was totally stunned by this. It was so unlike him, and he could come up with absolutely no reason for the depression. He began to indicate that his life was worthless and that he would never be able to "become anybody." He despaired that his life would ever amount to anything. Often he would say to me, "If it were not for hurting you so badly, I sure would like to die."

As this discouragement and depression continued, I tried repeatedly to get him to open up to another godly man/pastor/friend. He had a lot of issues dealing with guilt, and I would encourage him to find a man he could trust and with whom he could share his concerns. But Leon did not trust anybody for this. He felt he knew more than anybody else and his standard answer was, "What could he say to me that I don't already know?"

What a puzzle Leon's depression was to me. Prior to his 1982 breakdown, depression and an unwillingness to go for help were the only indications I had that things were not as A-OK with Leon as I had been believing. But after his breakdown, a strangeness even more mystifying began to manifest. He experienced severe sleeplessness and would create an atmosphere of feverish hyperactivity through the night hours. His visions of grandeur energized him hour after hour as he sought to attain unreachable and unreasonable goals.

In earlier chapters I attempt to establish the credibility of my godly pastor/missionary/Bible teacher/author husband. The next chapters will attempt to portray a picture of utter chaos due to his episodic behavior. The years that followed his initial breakdown consisted, time and again, of confinement to psychiatric clinics, loss of ministry position, grief, depression, death to his vision, loss of some friends, misunderstanding, shame and embarrassment, working at minimum wage jobs in place of using his Christian ministry training, and the list goes on.

Chapter 9

Help! Doesn't Anyone Understand?

L ooking up into his wild, blue eyes, his grip tightening around my throat, I managed to shout "JESUS!!" In one brief moment of release, I pulled away, darted for the front door and yelled "HELP!"

Thirty two years earlier, on a beautiful August evening in a church filled with some five hundred guests, I had stood looking into those same blue eyes, this time filled with love, as he held my hands and sang so beautifully, "Together With Jesus, Life's Pathway We Tread."

What had gone wrong? To answer this question, we need to fill in the events following the 1982 breakdown revealed in the previous chapter.

As I had not yet heard anything about manic depression, I was still trying to figure everything out from a spiritual basis. This explains why, after Leon had been at the hospital only a few days, some friends encouraged me to go with them and demand his release. This we did, blatantly disregarding medical advice. We were convinced we could get him home and that by speaking prayers and scriptures over him he would be "delivered."

Slowly Leon became functional once again, finding employment in a nearby mill. Eventually a friend at church helped get him a very good job in the mailroom of a large company. Life was progressing fairly smoothly and we pretty much put aside the horrible craziness that had occurred. While we were so thankful he could be employed, he desperately missed using his Bible teaching and pastoral gifts.

Imagine our joy when Leon was approached about taking a pastorate in Lusk, a small Wyoming town. To give up the two story home we had recently bought to move into a pastorate was not any kind of sacrifice. I was thrilled for Leon to have this opportunity, and he was overjoyed to once again be doing what he was trained for. The church was quite a challenge with its history of problems, but we worked diligently and lovingly to see relationships being restored and the church built up.

Alas! It was all too good to be true. After two years of ministry, just when things were going beautifully, Leon suffered another mini- breakdown. He spent a few weeks in the veterans hospital at Hot Springs, South Dakota. Upon his release the church board decided their pastor needed a little vacation. Since a very special party honoring my Mother was to take place in Los Angeles, we decided to drive out and spend our vacation in California.

As our holiday progressed, I began to get alarmed at Leon's strange behavior. He was not sleeping at night, was hyperactive, and was talking about wanting to go down to Mexico to "help the poor." He was not making sense. Any resistance or show of concern from me brought anger and threats of violence from him. I was becoming quite fearful. Thus, when Leon actually ordered me to fly on back to Wyoming and that he would come later with the car I had mixed feelings. At first I resisted because I was afraid of what might happen to him if I were not with him, but he actually forced me to leave on the airplane.

I returned to the parsonage at Lusk and waited to hear from Leon. He would make quick calls and never let me know exactly where he was. From both his manner and content of speech I knew something was very very wrong. We eventually pieced it together that he was living a most bizarre life on the streets of Los Angeles and that he was in a terrible mental condition.

Understandably, I was asked to vacate the parsonage as by now the church board knew Leon could not return as pastor. I was not given much warmth or understanding. How could they understand? I certainly did not! The people who knew my husband seemed to believe that this formerly great man of God had surely fallen into the depths of sin and was to be avoided.

About this time I did begin to learn about a disorder called "bipolar, manic depression." But it was frustrating to try to explain to others something I didn't fully understand myself. In those years there was much stigma attached to this illness. One did not choose to claim having a family member so diagnosed.

Eventually Leon was located in Los Angeles and once again committed to a mental hospital. Meanwhile, I drove my son Eugene's car to Oregon while he drove the van filled with all of my things. Since Eugene was scheduled to begin classes at a local Bible college, he offered to find an apartment and live with me instead of staying at the college dorm.

I immediately began looking for work so as to help keep a roof over my head. There was also the matter of negotiating with the car pound in Los Angeles that had confiscated our car which Leon had been "living" in while wandering the streets. I was finally able to come up with the money, go down to L.A. to recover our car and drive it back. The heartbreak of that trip was unbelievable, for attempting to visit my beloved husband in the mental hospital resulted in his total rejection of me. I had to work diligently to separate the sickness from the man. The man I married and had lived so happily with for some twenty five years loved me totally, was morally impeccable, kind and tender.

Driving back to Oregon with a heavy heart, I wondered what our future held. Surely the Lord Who so obviously brought us together was able to keep us together in spite of the present circumstances. How thankful I am for genuinely loving friends who rallied around my son and me and whose prayers brought us so much encouragement. One lady in particular took it upon herself to ply me with powerful scriptures from God's Word. She gave me specific assignments to read and speak His words aloud daily. Not willing to see me "go under" during this stressful period, she even checked up on me daily to make me accountable to her. What a blessing to have such a friend!

While I was adjusting to a new life in Oregon, Leon was responding to the hospital treatment in Los Angeles and was eventually released. But when I met him at the bus station, I was aware that he was still very different from the man I had married. He spent his days wandering around the streets in a highly manic state. Eugene and I both had reason to be wary and even fearful, and before long the police picked him up and soon he was back in a veterans hospital – this time in Roseburg, Oregon. To spare the reader endless details, suffice it to say that from June of 1986 to April of 1987 he was admitted 6 times to mental hospitals.

Chapter 10

Off To A Great
Start – But Then!!

G iven Leon's record, obtaining work was a pretty daunting task. But eventually he was hired as a Certified Nurses Assistant, going to homes to care for physically disabled people. His self esteem was very low, and he no longer had any hope of serving in Christian ministries.

Together, we managed to find employment as live- in apartment managers, and then as caregivers for Alzheimers patients. We were quite thankful to have adequate living quarters, well balanced meals and even a little income while assisting the residents in our care home. Yet my heart hurt for Leon knowing he longed to use his God-given spiritual gifts of teaching and preaching. He was by now stable, appropriate, and we were enjoying the love we had become so used to in earlier years.

During the next four years while recovering, we often wondered if we were now "on the shelf" as far as using the ministry gifts we had previously enjoyed. But our love for each other held strong, as did our love for and commitment to the Lord Jesus Christ.

Then, in late 1990 the light at the end of the tunnel
shone, and we found ourselves returning to full-time
Christian ministry. My high school friend, Jo, and her
husband, Malcolm Lee, were directors of a Rescue Mission
in Richmond, California, and they invited us to be a part of
their staff. Leon had the awesome responsibility of devel-
oping the Department of Biblical Studies – a systematic
program of college-level classes for men who had stumbled
into the Mission, turned their life over to Christ, and shown
a desire to be trained in His Word. I was handed the leader-
ship at Shiloh House – a nine month training program for
single mothers who desired to break the cycle of poverty
and learn independent living skills.

For the next three years, Leon and I were vibrantly alive
with the joy of serving God in what is known in Richmond
as "the iron triangle" of the San Francisco Bay Area. Truly
an inpoverished part of California with 89% of its 7,000
residents being unemployed. It was a great joy to distribute
monthly food boxes, household supplies and to provide
beds for 130 people every night. With San Quentin prison
being so close by, Leon had the privilege of preaching there
several times. He also teamed up regularly with Malcolm
Lee to co-host "Night Talk", an all-night TV program.
Another ministry he loved was that of volunteer "pastor"
within a mainline church to a group of Laotians, teaching
them through an interpreter.

Alas, this was all too good to be true. As "happy stress"
escalated with the joy and excitement of ministry, Leon
once again began showing frightening signs of imbalance. Indeed, his flight of ideas led him to wander about
the town, and inappropriate behavior began to manifest.
Considering the level of Leon's spiritual visibility, it
became obvious that he must be restrained so as to not
cause confusion to the many folk who looked up to him. It
seemed to me, unthinkable that it should happen again. I

thought of the precious babes in Christ and what they now saw and heard from their "Pastor Leon." I, of course, realized he desperately needed to be hospitalized. The mental health system being what it is, nothing could be done to retain him or to force him to get medical help unless he committed a crime.

The visions of grandeur Leon was experiencing prompted him to take our car and drive up to Oregon. Here he ran into much opposition and seemed to be at a loss as to know where to go next. The rescue mission could not have been more loving, kind or generous in every way. They never asked that we leave. But I saw no other choice – too much damage had been done, and it seemed best for us to flee that area. Thus, Malcolm Lee handed me money for a bus ticket to go up to Oregon and find my husband. The Mission graciously volunteered to pack up all of our belongings and bring them to Oregon as soon as I notified them of storage facilities.

And so ended our heretofore delightfully happy, meaningful and fulfilling stint at the Richmond Rescue Mission!

Chapter 11

How Much Stress
Can One Body Take?

This next phase was, for me, one of the most difficult I have ever experienced. I remember saying to Leon when he was recovering from his mental breakdown at Roseburg VA Hospital, "Honey, I really don't think my body can handle any more of this." He had been expressing his gratefulness for my strength and ability to always "be there" in his time of need. But I wondered how much longer I would be able to hold up. We were to soon find out.

It began with my literally collapsing on the front porch of "City of Refuge," a women's shelter where I was taken by some loving Christians who I met soon after I arrived in Oregon. During this time, Leon was finally "captured," so to speak, and taken once again to a mental hospital to receive the obviously much-needed medication to bring him "down." At the same time, I began to notice some regular bleeding which indicated only one thing: Cancer. Since we were by now deeply in financial debt, and since I was far too weak to try to even go out and look for employment, I chose to say nothing to the staff at the shelter and to keep my situation a secret. I was at such a level of despair by now that I concluded dying from cancer would be more pleasant than continuing to live.

After a few weeks, I felt emotionally strong enough to venture out to Salem and seek employment through Goodwill Temporary Services. I was given the position of data entry operator in Oregon's Department of Justice. I also approached the director of Samaritan's Inn (a Christian facility offering transitional housing for men) to see if they would allow my husband to fill their position as Resident Manager/Cook. Leon was ready to be released from the hospital, but they would not allow his release until he had housing.

Position granted, this became a very good situation for Leon and me to live together in a cozy one room cottage, for me to continue my job in the Salem office, and for Leon to not only cook dinner at "the main house," but also to lead a weekly Bible study for the men. His gifts soon became apparent, and the men began to seek his counsel and his prayers.

Up to now I had kept my "little secret" even from Leon – but due to a plumbing problem, he discovered blood in the toilet one day when he used it after I had been there. Visibly upset, he demanded to know how long this had been going on, and he exclaimed we had to get to a hospital immediately. I cried out, "No, no, we can't get further in debt. And we have no insurance."

However, in God's providence, I soon received notice from GTS that I had now accrued the required number of employment hours to be fully covered through GTS with an excellent Kaiser Health Plan. That same day Leon made an appointment for me to be seen.

By this time, the tumor had grown to what the doctor termed "the size of a basketball," and he claimed I measured "the size of an 8 month pregnant woman." I was pretty much told that the cancer would by now have gone throughout my system, that they would remove the tumor and send me home to – you guessed it - to die. Of course from the moment my husband discovered the blood, he began to lay hands on me for prayer, and he went up to the altar with me at church services for more healing prayer. My children all said their "goodbyes," and my sister had me flown down to Los Angeles for "closure" with her and other family members. Meanwhile, as the cancer grew inside of me, I had the most beautiful peace, remaining calm and full of God's promises.

On August 24, 1994 I went under the knife for almost 8 hours while a 10 inch ovarian mass was removed, plus a cancerous kidney that was discovered during surgery. A few days later, the pathology report came back "There is no evidence of residual tumor." The doctor said, "You are a very, very lucky lady." Leon and I listened respectfully to the advice of the oncologist, read the materials offered, prayed earnestly, and then chose not to take any chemo therapy or radiation. On October 4, I returned to my 40 hour week position at Department of Justice.

Chapter 12

Hopes Go Up In Smoke

The announcement that Samaritan's Inn was going through a management change and that staff was to be rearranged sent Leon and me once again to our knees to claim God's housing provision. In God's delightful way of leading His children, we decided one bright sunny day to drive down to Eugene, Oregon to visit with our son Raymond. On our return trip, when we once again passed the "Living Rock Museum" sign Leon had seen so often on I-5, he said, "I've always wanted to go see that. How about today?" We turned east and in a few short miles we arrived in Brownsville and entered the driveway of a fairly large house with an adjoining uniquely shaped rock house. Being a genuine rock lover, Leon found the museum more than a little bit fascinating, and soon the builder's daughter invited us into the home and began asking questions.

As it turned out, this daughter and her sister (who lived in homes a few miles away) were at that very time praying and wondering who they might get to come and live in the big house while also serving as a tour guide. Tears came to our eyes when we exclaimed that at this very time we were praying and wondering where we might find housing! It was a perfect fit!

Our daughter and granddaughter were so thrilled when Christmas time came and they flew out from Arizona to spend the holidays with us. Our little Rendell Family was now complete when Eugene and his wife and Raymond with some of his friends showed up at our house. How thrilled we were to have this special time together. We had no idea when taking a group picture that we would never again be so assembled!

After all the other guests had left, Sharnelle and I were in the living room pouring over a stack of family photo albums, and little Roseanne was down the hall drawing in one of the bedrooms. Sharnelle begged her dad to light a fire in the fireplace just so that she could go back to Phoenix and brag about spending Christmas in the snow and with a fireplace.

Things did not go as planned, and due to a mishap, the fire got out of control, the curtain windows lit up, and we were racing to get Roseanne and all of us out of the house. Suddenly, my darling little granddaughter began to cry, "Woody! Mommy, Woody is inside!!" A nearby volunteer heard this, braved the flames, ran in and found Roseanne's beloved "Toy Story" doll, Woody! As Brownsville is a very small town, it was only a matter minutes before several fire fighters had arrived and managed to snuff out the flames.

During the weeks that followed, as we spent our days cleaning up the mess, and our nights accepeting housing with friends, Leon believed he did not want to continue staying in the Brownsville home. Indeed, he had been getting far too much pressure from the owners regarding the upkeep, and pressure is something that people with his disorder find difficult to cope with.

Again, in God's providence, a couple who had invited us over one night for dinner told us about their daughter and husband in Tonala (near Guadalajara Mexico) who were praying for a retired couple to come assist them in their ministry. By this time we were receiving a monthly disability check for Leon which was definitely not sufficient for us to maintain housing in America, but would be plenty to live on in Mexico. We prayed about it, decided to drive to Mexico and check this out. If working with this couple did not seem mutually right, then we would simply find a place in Mexico and live as God's servants in that land – doing whatever we could to help the local body of Christ. And so begins our Mexico saga.

Chapter 13

Life Goes South, South Of The Border

It was early February, 1996 when we left Oregon, bound for a new life in Mexico! All of our earthly belongings had either been (1) packed into every nook and cranny of our car, (2) sold, (3) given away, or as in the case of precious photo albums, (4)stored with family members. Our two sons sent us off with their love and prayers as we headed first for Arizona to spend time with our daughter and family.

Little did we realize when Sharnelle served up her Daddy's 54th birthday cake during that visit that it would be his last! It was so precious having that time together with her. We learned later that she and a couple of her friends were hoping to make a trip to visit us in our new place of residence. But sudden death changed all of that!

By the time we got to El Paso, I was having serious concerns as to Leon's stability. I saw frightening signs of imbalance: agitation, irritability, driving in city streets almost like a maniac, reckless spending and charging unnecessary items far beyond our budget, insomnia and pacing about feverishly all through the night. I was afraid to cross the border with him like this, because I had seen it all before and knew he was definitely on the edge of serious psychotic behavior.

I managed to get him into the waiting room of the V.A hospital in El Paso where he exhibited more uncharacteristic and strange behavior. Yet the examining physician intoned what we'd often heard: "He is neither a threat to himself nor to society. We cannot commit him." She was deaf to our literal cries and pleas for help. Leon was still well enough to realize he needed help.

There was nothing we could do at this point except to cross over the border and hope to get safely into the shelter of the American missionaries in Guadalajara who were expecting us.

I was quite fearful by now, and Leon's mental imbalance had begun to escalate to the point where he felt he was invincible and could drive the car even though he had misplaced his glasses in the previous night's frenzy. We had some near misses, and finally I convinced him to relinquish the wheel with soothing words such as, "Honey, you are really getting tired. I'll help you by driving awhile. You just take a little nap." It worked!

His speech was becoming more and more pressured, especially as he expressed one grandiose thought after another. It was important for me to remain outwardly calm, as though I were in agreement. About 45 minutes from the USA border, Leon shouted, "Honey! STOP the car! There is gold in the street. God has provided for us!!" We were on a divided highway that had a paved border in the middle. I pulled the car into that border, stopped, and Leon got out and lay face down on the pavement almost weeping with joy that "God has provided this gold for us!" He then instructed me to continue driving on into the next town to buy some food because "I cannot leave this gold."

Unless the reader has personally dealt with someone in such a psychotic, delusional state, it may be difficult to understand how forceful and possibly violent one can become if ones orders are not followed. I was, by this time, well aware of such danger. Beyond that, I was also unspeakably weary from the strain of being in close proximity to Leon while he was like this. I actually welcomed the prospect of a short reprieve, getting a little bite of lunch for myself in peace and quiet, and finding a phone to alert my family of urgent need to pray.

I drove approximately 2 miles into the next town, called my family, ate a quick sandwich and ordered take out for my husband. I was gone for less than thirty minutes, but when I returned Leon was nowhere in sight. I reasoned that since he had been expressing such joy about going down to Guadalajara he would not have turned back towards the border. I then concluded he must have become impatient and walked or hitchhiked toward the town I had been in.

Retracing my tracks, I went up to each farm house, into all of the businesses on the edge of town, asking if they recognized the picture I showed of my husband. Finally I went to the police station with my concern. Of course by this time I was frantic and tears were flowing. A kind Mexican who spoke good English escorted me to a motel where, in Spanish, he explained it all to the desk clerk, and then I was taken to a room to rest. The police put out a bulletin to be on the lookout for my husband.

The next morning I was told to relax and wait while they continued to search for Leon. But in a couple of hours I decided to continue my drive south, which I did – stopping in each city to inquire at police stations. By this time I reasoned that he had been hitchhiking and that when I got to Guadalajara I would find him.

It was not to be. It was also awkward and embarrassing to try to explain to suspicious American missionaries at my destination – people we had never met before – that my husband had disappeared. You see, at that time mental illness was something not clearly understood by the general population. Imagine my humiliation to have these strangers (folk Leon and I had anticipated working, worshipping, ministering with) insinuate that my husband and I really must have had a terrible falling out and that he had left me! I wept alone in their guest bedroom.

Since Leon did not show up at our planned destination, I now reasoned that he must have turned back toward the border and may actually be back in America. I made several calls trying to discover what had happened to him. Finally, I learned from the very same VA Hospital in El Paso who had turned Leon away when he pled to be admitted, that the police had found him wandering the streets of their city and had brought him to that ward.

Since my car had broken down and I had to wait for parts to be ordered from America, I had to spend several days in the hostile environment mentioned above. Thankfully, during those days a lovely couple who had been missionaries in Calera, Mexico came to visit my hosts. This couple was so kind and understanding, listening with compassion to my story.

It also turned out that they were actually in the process of moving from Calera to Guadalajara. How God provided for me through them was amazing. By this time I, of course, did not feel welcome with the missionaries we thought we were coming to work with. But my new friends from Calera invited me to return with them, introduce me to their landlord who they were certain would be delighted to have another reliable American renting their house, and assist me with the initial moving in business matters. They were also eager to have me meet Rafael and his wonderful Christian family who lived right across the street from their house and who spoke very good English.

Oh, what a blessing this was! Now I knew Leon and I would have a lovely house to live in, great neighbors, and an opportunity to do in Calera what we truly wanted to do somewhere in Mexico: Be of support and encouragement to the local body of believers. The landlord was quite happy to rent to me, even without meeting Leon.

So much time had now elapsed, that Leon was transferred from the El Paso hospital to a facility in Albuquerque, New Mexico. So I had to now make not only the 17 hour drive up to the border, but then on to Albuquerque. No problem! I was about to be joined with my precious husband who I knew had by now been treated with drugs that would have brought him back down to reality. I knew, too, that his lithium level would be such that there should no longer be signs of chemical imbalance.

What I did not know was that in his sick state he had concluded, while prostrate on the pavement, laying claim to "all that gold," I had apparently abandoned him. He had gotten up and tried to flag motorists to stop, but his appearance and behavior was such that drivers sped fearfully right past him. Finally, he literally threw himself on the hood of a truck that slowed down a bit! The frightened driver reluctantly gave him a ride across the border and then let him out. He created more than one "scene" before the police finally got him to the hospital.

The mindset that I had truly left Leon on the pavement to die and had traveled on toward our given destination without him was still very much a part of my husband's delusional thinking when he was told I was coming to Albuquerque. When word of this came to me, I begged the doctor, "Please, please do not release him until you are sure he is balanced. I know he is safe with you, and I am coming to get him."

When I did arrive in Albuquerque, I first located a women's shelter and received permission to stay there indefinitely until my husband was released. Meanwhile, my daily visits to be with Leon at the hospital were somewhat strained. It was obvious he was not yet quite himself, and it took time and patience on my part to eventually convince him of my enduring love and that there never was for one minute a thought on my part to abandon him.

Chapter 14

Safely Hospsitalized

With each psychotic episode, followed by restraints, forced drugging, hospital restriction, and then slow recovery from the initially administered heavy drugs, I noticed a pattern of negative changes in my husband. I felt saddened by the obvious toll all of this took on him. I never once had a doubt that "my Leon" totally loved the Lord Jesus and that his heart burned within him to follow and serve the Lord. But I also realized that this insidious mental illness was trying to rob Leon of spiritual effectiveness.

I knew by now that for the rest of our life together, my job would be to watch over Leon and to lovingly protect him from stress. I realized that he could no longer take any position of responsibility where he was expected to be and to perform on a regular basis. But I also knew that in a calm, stable mental state he could and would be a tremendous blessing and encouragement to local pastors and leaders in the land where we were now going to live.

This was my thinking during the long drive, retracing our path down into Mexico. Leon was impressed and thankful to learn that I had rented a house we could move into. We were by now into the month of March, and Leon had not forgotten that my birthday was on the 31st. When we arrived in Calera, he was so thrilled with the lovely, spacious house, with our good neighbors, and with the fun of planning a party for me.

The day dawned bright and joyous with Leon plucking a rose from our beautiful gardens and bringing it to my bedside! He was very, very happy. I did not yet understand that there was such a thing as "happy stress" that is as capable of triggering an imbalance as is "bad stress." Later that day our new neighbors gathered several of their friends to come to the party and help us celebrate.

The next nine days are almost too bizarre, even too painful, for me to put into writing. Leon's behavior not only became inappropriate, but dangerous. His speech portrayed unrealistic ideas that prompted me to not only hide our passports and checkbook, but also to drive our car and park it in a hidden spot and then hide the keys. I lived in constant fear as to what strange thing he was going to try to do next. His imbalance was rapidly escalating, and on more than one occasion I feared for my own life due to his wild accusations and demands. I found out firsthand the power and the victory that is available to use when we simply cry out to JESUS.

Rafael and his family assisted me in contacting local doctors for help. Soon I was able to convince Leon to get into our car and let me take him to a hospital where he could "get a good rest." In actuality, it was a mental hospital in Zacataces where the staff was well aware that a wild eyed, loud and very strange behaving American man was being brought in. On the drive to Zacatecas, Leon was so far gone that he was literally babbling nonsensically. When we arrived, I finally got him to get out of the car where he then proceeded to sit down on the curb, weeping like a baby. I kept assuring him, "Honey, I won't let anything bad happen to you. Just come in with me and you will feel so much better."

I saw some of the hospital staff peering out of the entryway. As I finally cajoled Leon to stand up and begin letting me support and walk him into the building, I noticed one nurse after another discreetly motion for me to follow, and as we walked down long halls and into adjacent wings, I would hear one door after another close and lock behind us. Meanwhile, I kept up an attempt to murmur calmly about the lovely plants we passed, the pretty murals on the walls, etc.

We finally got to the appointed destination, where Leon was asked to sit down. He looked up at me with great fear in his eyes and I said, "I'm right here, Honey. I won't let them do a thing to hurt you. You are going to feel so much better." I kept that up all the while they finally got him to swallow a couple of very strong pills.

In a very short time, Leon calmed down and we were led into an adjoining dining area where other patients were having lunch. We ate some food and then Leon was led into a little room of his own to lie down on the bed. The drug (I believe it was Haldol) quickly brought "my Leon" back, and he appeared relaxed and even at peace with himself as he lay on the bed with me sitting close beside him. The private conversation he and I then had remains forever etched in my mind and heart.

Chapter 15

Time To Go Home

A t this point I was 100% certain that life as I had
known it for 32 plus years was about to change
in a way that I felt would be totally unacceptable. That
is, I knew my life was no longer safe with Leon, that he
was now cycling increasingly fast and furiously, and that
drastic measures had to be taken concerning our future
living arrangements. It was also quite apparent that he and
I needed to leave Mexico. Any thought of his having credibility to be of spiritual help to the believers there was now
clouded with confusion by folk who did not understand
mental illness.

All of these thoughts were swirling about in my head
when suddenly Leon, who now began to understand how
dark the situation had become, announced brightly, "Oh
Honey, I know what we can do. We'll move up to White
City, Oregon where there is a domiciliary for veterans. I
certainly qualify to live there. They do not allow civilian
mates to reside in the "dom." but you could get an apartment in White City and we could see each other every day."

I continued my brave act of appearing cheerful and
agreeable, when in my heart I knew that to live separately

from him was something I could not even consider. I was thinking to myself, "What kind of a marriage would that be? He in the VA facility, and me in an apartment by myself." But I saw absolutely no solution to the dilemma. So I just went along with him in a cheery manner. I knew that the US Embassy would assist us in our return to America as I had already been in contact with them. They were well aware of Leon's condition and promised to help whenever needed.

After a little while of visiting together, I looked at my watch and told Leon I needed to get into town and put money down for an appliance to be delivered to the house. The store was about to close for the day, so he and I prepared to say our goodbyes.

And now here is the sweetest part to that afternoon's conversation that I can still hear and visualize. Leon held my hands, looked at me so tenderly, and said, "Norma, I have put you through SO much. But you have never left me. You have always been here for me through it all." With tender love I assured him, "And my precious Leon, I am not leaving you now. Somehow we are going to make it!" We kissed and parted with the last words he and I would ever speak to each other on this earth, "See you in the morning."

Yes indeed. I will see Jerold Leon Romprey on that bright and glorious morning when the Lord Jesus calls me home!

I took care of finalizing the purchase, returned to our house in Calera and enjoyed a peaceful sleep, uninterrupted by the agitated, maniacal actions of a very sick husband. My first such sleep in eight hellish days. Days filled with events I cannot bring myself to think on long enough to express them in writing. Trust me, I was experiencing constant, fearful stress. So it was indeed a welcome relief to know that I was safe in my bed and that Leon was comfortable, safe and being taken care of in his bed at the hospital.

At 6:30 AM. the shrill ring of the telephone awoke me. It was Rafael from across the street saying, "Leon died this morning."

With a sad and heavy heart, and while holding the box containing Leon's ashes, I headed once again up that long 17 hour drive to the border where I met my sister who so lovingly had come to accompany me on up to Los Angeles.

It was in one of the motel rooms of the Narramore Christian Foundation, then in Rosemead, California, where my sister was Hostess and her husband was Grounds Keeper, that my 3 children found me clutching the wooden box containing all that was now left of our loved one.

A special memorial to honor his life was held in the NCF chapel. From there we drove on to Oregon where all 3 of my children and many friends gave support as we had a burial of Leon's remains in a Portland national cemetery.

<u>Conclusion</u>

NO!, Mz. Talk Show Host. I absolutely do NOT buy it!

There is, <u>indeed</u>, such a thing as Bi-Polar Chemical Disorder.

I lived with it first hand.

To all who looked and listened in shock disbelief as

Leon J. Rendell

exhibited manic behavior,

I had this to say:

"Yes, that is the <u>*voice*</u> of Leon,

But it is the *illness* that is speaking.

Yes, those are the <u>*limbs*</u> of Leon,

But it is the *illness* that is acting out."

D ear reader, are you going through a difficult time? Are you being maligned or ridiculed because of an illness or a disorder that others seem to misunderstand? As I look back upon those years of living with my beloved Leon through long periods of devastation, I am reminded of God's sustaining power and of the words written in Isaiah 43:2 (The Message.) May you, too, find comfort, strength and endurance to endure to the end.

"Don't be afraid.
I've redeemed you!
I've called your name. You're mine.

When you're in over your head, I'll be there with you.
When you're in rough waters, you will not go down.
When you're between a rock and a hard place, it won't be a dead end....

Because
I am God, your personal God, The Holy of Israel, your Savior!!"